DATE VIOLENCE

Elaine Landau

Franklin Watts
A Division of Scholastic Inc.
New York • Toronto • London • Auckland • Sydney
Mexico City • New Delhi • Hong Kong
Danbury, Connecticut

Dedication

*For Megan Gannon, an outstanding
educator and principal*

Cover design by John Gibson.
Interior design by Kathleen Santini.

Library of Congress Cataloging-in-Publication Data

Landau, Elaine.
    Date violence / Elaine Landau.
        v. cm. — (Life balance)
    Includes bibliographical references and index.
    Contents: At first glance—Dating violence—Date rape—Questions
    and answers about dating violence—Glossary.
        ISBN 0-531-12214-X (lib. bdg.)   0-531-16613-9 (pbk.)
        1. Dating violence—Juvenile literature. 2. Date rape—Juvenile lit-
    erature. 3. Dating violence—Prevention—Juvenile literature. 4. Date
    rape—Prevention—Juvenile literature. [1. Dating violence. 2. Date
    rape. 3. Questions and answers.] I. Title. II. Series.
        HQ801.83.L36 2004
        362.88—dc22
                                                2003019480

Table of Contents

One

When Love Turns Ugly

Terri had known for a while that her relationship with her boyfriend, Johnny, wasn't perfect. He had a temper and could be quite demanding. Yet everything fell apart one Saturday when Johnny rang Terri's doorbell at noon and announced that they were going out. They weren't supposed to go out until later that night, and because both of her parents worked on Saturday, Terri had to watch her five-year-old twin sisters. She explained the situation to Johnny, but he didn't care. He wanted to drive down to the beach with Terri. She asked if the twins could come, but Johnny said that he didn't want to be a nanny.

She knew that her parents would be furious if she left the twins alone, but she couldn't say no to Johnny. He waited in the car while she got ready to go. Leaving wasn't as easy as she had hoped. One of the twins started crying, and the other demanded to know who was going to make their lunch. Through all this commotion, Johnny was outside blowing the car horn. As the honks got longer, Terri could sense Johnny's growing anger.

Just as she was on her way out, she heard Johnny scream from his car, "Get out here, you stupid, crazy idiot!" At that instant Terri wished that she could fall into a hole and bury herself. She knew that if she heard Johnny, everyone else on the block heard him, too.

He had called her names before in private, but Terri had always made an excuse for him. She'd tell herself that he didn't mean it or that he was just upset about something. Often she blamed herself for provoking him, thinking that it was all her fault or that she somehow wasn't good enough for Johnny.

But when her treasured boyfriend humiliated her in front of all the neighbors, she knew that Johnny was wrong. She also knew that she had almost made a terrible mistake in leaving the twins alone just to please him. Terri decided that she would not be going after all.

When she walked out of the house to tell him so, she found Johnny leaning against his car. He didn't apologize;

he simply said, "It's about time. Get in the car." Gathering up all her courage, Terri told Johnny that she wasn't going. She added that she wanted him to apologize for the name-calling.

Terri had turned to go back into the house when Johnny grabbed her arm, spun her around, and slapped her face hard. Terri lost her balance and fell on the sidewalk. Johnny got in his car and drove off, calling out, "You ugly, stupid pile of garbage. You don't deserve someone like me." He sped away, leaving Terri where she had landed on the sidewalk. Both twins had seen what happened from the window and were crying harder than ever.

The Forms of Abuse

Terri was a victim of date violence. As in Terri's case, date violence usually does not occur as an isolated incident. It is often a pattern of abuse that ultimately makes the victim feel less human. That Saturday, Terri was hit, yelled at, and called names, but dating violence can encompass still more. It is frequently defined as physically, emotionally, or sexually harming someone you are dating.

Date violence is frequently defined as physically, emotionally, or sexually harming someone you are dating.

Physical Abuse

Physical abuse can take many forms. People do not necessarily have to have their nose broken or their teeth knocked out to experience it. Physical abuse can be more subtle yet still extremely hurtful. In date-violence cases, physical abuse can include pinching, restraining, kicking, choking, pushing, shoving, slapping, biting, burning, and hair pulling. Often the violence escalates as the abuser becomes familiar with how much he or she can get away with. Terri had allowed Johnny to insult her and call her names before he slapped her and left her lying on the sidewalk. If she continued her relationship with him, it's likely that things would get worse.

Emotional Abuse

The most obvious forms of emotional abuse include insults, threats, humiliation, and yelling to frighten or intimidate someone. Emotional abuse also occurs when individuals try to control their girlfriend's or boyfriend's movements, destroy his or her property, or isolate him or her from family and friends, making the person feel powerless and alone. Emotional abuse can be more difficult to recognize and identify than physical abuse because it does not leave visible scars or bruises. Remember the saying "Sticks and stones will break my bones but names will never hurt me?" Don't believe it—name-calling hurts. Though Terri didn't see it at first, Johnny was a master at emotional abuse. The insults, yelling, and public humiliation all served to make Terri feel worthless and undeserving.

Sexual Abuse

Sexual abuse includes forced sex or being made to perform unwanted sexual acts. Other forms of sexual abuse are using the threat of force, refusing to use a condom, and unwanted touching. In date-violence situations females have sometimes endured sexual abuse in order to avoid physical or severe emotional abuse. In other cases, boys have made girls feel that they owe them sex because they paid for them on a date or because they've gone out with them for a long time. But paying for dates is not the same thing as buying sex, and dating someone for months or even years does not give anyone a pass to "go all the way."

Terri's Story

What happened to Terri is not as unusual as most people would like to believe. While the whole idea behind dating may be to find a loving and fun person to be with, some-times it doesn't work out that way. Instead, some young people are abused by people who are supposed to care about them.

Of course, it doesn't always start out this way. At first glance, almost any girl would have wanted to be Terri. She was Johnny's girl, and he was the guy almost every girl wanted. Johnny was not only gorgeous, but he was also president of the senior class, captain of the football team, and the most popular boy at school. Now that Terri had Johnny, people saw her in a different light. It was as if some of his fabulousness had rubbed off on her.

Terri had never thought of herself as fabulous, not even now that she was Johnny's girl. She didn't know why he had picked her and sometimes couldn't believe her good fortune. He called her his angel and his blue-eyed beauty, and he even said that her freckles were cute. When they walked into a party and Johnny had his arm around her, Terri felt as though she had won the lottery. That's how it was at first, anyway.

In time, though, Terri began to see another side of Johnny. Johnny was a real "he-man" type, and when they began dating, Terri considered that a plus. She liked being with someone strong who wasn't afraid to take charge. She could tell that Johnny really cared for her, because he was extremely jealous. If anyone so much as looked at her, he went crazy. None of her other boyfriends had been that way, and Terri felt that this was what it must be like when someone really loves you. She was flattered beyond words.

Nevertheless, sometimes it got a little scary. Once, after a football game, Johnny thought he saw one of Terri's old boyfriends looking at her. He felt certain that her ex, Kevin, was still after Terri. Johnny glared at Kevin from the football field, cursing him under his breath. He told Terri that he wanted to kill Kevin and accused her of still liking him. It took Terri more than twenty minutes to calm Johnny down. She had to repeatedly assure him that Kevin, who was with another girl that day, was not interested in her. Terri finally managed to smooth things over, but it wasn't easy.

Riding home from the game that day, Terri realized that being Johnny's girlfriend was a lot of work. Terri always had to be careful not to get him angry. The slightest thing could set him off, so it was like walking on eggshells. Terri had to be sure that she was sufficiently flattering to Johnny as well. He never tired of hearing how great he was. In some ways, Terri had become his personal cheerleader.

Though she never told anyone, Terri also thought that Johnny was a bit of a bully. He liked things done his way and made it clear that no girlfriend of his would ever challenge him on anything. It was obvious that Johnny wanted to be in control. After a few months of dating, Terri felt as if she were losing part of herself. Johnny wanted to be the center of her universe. But Terri's universe had been pretty full before she ever went out with him. Now Terri was required to make Johnny her top priority.

After a few months of dating, Terri felt as if she were losing part of herself. Johnny wanted to be the center of her universe. But Terri's universe had been pretty full before she ever went out with him.

As time passed, Johnny became increasingly impatient. He'd blow up at Terri for no reason, sometimes simply because he didn't like the look on her face. If she'd dropped something when they were first dating, he'd rush to pick it up for her. Now he just called her clumsy. Johnny also made tremendous demands on Terri's time. Terri had always excelled in math and had been picked by the school's faculty to work in the peer tutoring program. She enjoyed tutoring others, but Johnny insisted that she give it up. He didn't like that some of the students Terri worked with were boys. He also wanted her to be available to him at all times.

After Johnny left that Saturday, Terri put her feelings aside long enough to comfort the twins. Terri surprised herself. She thought that she'd be beside herself over losing the most popular boy at school. Instead she felt a tremendous sense of relief. As she prepared her sisters' lunch, she started giggling. One of the twins asked her what was so funny, and Terri answered, "I was just thinking that Johnny was right. I don't deserve someone like him. I deserve better."

The story doesn't end here. Johnny decided to "forgive" Terri's "brat behavior," as he described it, and take her back. Terri was tempted to forgive him, but then she thought better of it. Wanting more for herself, Terri decided to pass on Johnny. She found the courage to leave the town's local wonder. She realized that the strength had always been inside her.

Terri made a wise decision. Despite how "desirable" her boyfriend was to the outside world, he had been abusive to her. Though Johnny had hit her only once, that was one time too many. No one ever deserves to be hit in a dating relationship.

Abusive Teen Relationships

The notion of abusive teen relationships is relatively new. Until recently, the majority of Americans thought of battered or abused people as being adult married women. The stereotype was that of a woman with young children whose husband dominated, humiliated, and hurt her. However, this is a narrow view of the situation. The range of people who become involved in these destructive relationships is actually much broader.

Studies show that violence among dating teens is as common as it is in adult marriages and live-in situations. According to *The Journal of the American Medical Association,* one survey in 2001 reported that at least one in every five high-school girls has dated a violent boy. Another study released in 2002 revealed that the rates could be even higher. This research on teen dating violence was conducted by researchers at the University of Arkansas. The results showed that fifty percent of the high-school students interviewed had experienced some form of physically violent behavior in their relationships.

In reporting the findings at an international conference held in New Hampshire, researcher Megan Mooney noted that teens who accept violent dating partners in high-school relationships often continue to date violent people later in life. "One of the reasons we should be concerned about dating violence in high schools is that it could be the beginning of a developmental trend, where young people become accustomed to experiencing and perpetuating violence with their partners, and they carry it into subsequent [future] relationships," explains Mooney. "[Date] violence has wide-ranging detrimental effects—physical, psychological, sociological, and economic—and this could be where it starts."

Date violence does not cut across just age lines. It also occurs in every type of neighborhood throughout the country. It exists in rural areas as well as in urban centers. It happens among rich people, poor people, and individuals of all races and ethnic groups. Gay and lesbian teens experience date violence as often as straight teens do.

Date violence happens among individuals of all races and ethnic groups. Gay and lesbian teens experience date violence as often as straight teens do.

In heterosexual (boy-girl) relationships, girls are not the only victims. Boys are victims of date violence, too. However, girls are more often the victims of violence. A recent National Crime Victimization Survey found that females are six times more likely than males to be abused by people they date. These findings are supported by U.S. Department of Justice statistics, which indicate that girls are abused both more frequently and more severely than boys.

Though teen date violence has only recently been recognized, it is not a new problem. There is nothing trendy about it. It has gone on for years. In 2000, the U.S. Department of Justice revealed that the highest rates for all types of violence in our society were experienced by those under the age of twenty-five. That's a frightening reality, and an important call for change.

When Boys Are Date-Violence Victims

People tend to think only of females as date-violence victims, but this is not the case. Though it happens to them less often, males can be victims as well. As Jan Brown, executive director and founder of the Domestic Abuse Hotline for Men, explains, "Domestic [or date] violence is not about size, gender, or strength."

However, males tend to be less likely than females to admit that they've been abused. The Domestic Abuse Hotline for Men cites the following reasons "why men don't tell":

- Many males cope with being abused by taking on a macho "I can handle it" attitude.

- They tell themselves that they've been hurt much worse on an athletic playing field. That is not the same thing as being physically attacked by someone they are dating, however, which hurts emotionally as well as physically.

- Males usually face more disbelief and ridicule than females do in this situation. This reinforces the tendency to remain silent about what's happening.

- Abusers are experts at making victims feel like no one is on their side. This makes the abused individual feel that there is no point in telling.

Two

A Pattern

of Abuse

Sixteen-year-old Liz was going to be a bridesmaid in her older sister's wedding. Like the other bridesmaids, she would wear a beautiful long-sleeved blue taffeta gown. The dress was the perfect color—it matched Liz's bruises and her black-and-blue eye.

The marks and skin discoloration were her boyfriend Zach's handiwork. Liz had been late meeting him, and Zach saw that as a sign of disrespect. Liz had not meant it to be. She was forced to stay late at her job after the girl on the next shift called in sick. Liz's boss had needed a little extra time to find a replacement, and Liz was unable to reach Zach to tell him.

When Liz finally arrived, Zach did not give her a chance to explain. He simply grabbed Liz's arm and twisted it behind her back. The pain was awful, and she wanted to cry out. But Liz knew that would only make Zach angrier. She couldn't stop the tears from welling up in her eyes, though. That may be why she didn't see Zach's fist coming toward her face. It was a fairly powerful punch, one that left Liz with a black eye.

Be Aware!

Even after Zach blackened Liz's eye, she didn't think of herself as having been abused. This isn't unusual. Sometimes young people suspect that their boyfriends or girlfriends aren't treating them as well as they should be, but they aren't sure what is wrong or why it is happening. In these cases, knowledge can be an especially valuable tool. It is important to be aware of the most common signs of dating abuse. Date violence is not a joke; it takes a heavy toll on the lives of numerous youths. Many become depressed and increasingly isolated from their friends and family. The following checklist lists

Sometimes young people suspect that their boyfriends or girlfriends aren't treating them as well as they should be, but they aren't sure what is wrong or why it is happening.

some of the warning signs of abuse. Does the person you are dating exhibit even one of these? If so, he or she is being abusive and is not someone you should be with.

Does he or she:

- make fun of you or humiliate you in front of your friends, classmates, or family?
- belittle or make light of your hopes, dreams, or achievements?
- criticize your decisions or views?
- tell you that you are worthless without him or her?
- blame you for his or her bad feelings or mistakes?
- pressure you for sex or force you to have sex?
- continually call you to make sure you are where you said you'd be?
- stalk you? This would involve secretly following you, waiting outside your home to see when you come and go, or simply "showing up" wherever you happen to be.
- treat you roughly, such as hitting, pushing, shoving, or grabbing you?
- tell you that you can't see your friends or insist that you put him or her above your family?

Zach insisted that Liz put him before her family, which often tore her apart. She felt that she continually had to lie and make excuses to keep both Zach and her parents happy. After Zach punched her, she had to make sure that her parents didn't find out. They never liked Zach and had not allowed Liz to invite him to her sister's wedding. If they knew that he hit her, Liz thought they'd call the police.

To explain her black eye, Liz told her mother that she was accidentally hit while playing volleyball in gym class. Liz's mother was horrified, but she believed the story. When the bruises still weren't gone by the day of the wedding, Liz had more cover-up work to do. The bruises on her arm were hidden under the dress. But her eye was still a problem. The only thing she could think to do was to wear sunglasses. That wasn't easy—the church was dimly lit, and Liz almost tripped as she walked down the aisle. Later, everyone asked her about the sunglasses, and she had to keep repeating the volleyball story. Though Liz hoped that no one would guess the truth, she felt sure that some people must have. When the wedding pictures later arrived, Liz didn't want to see them. She looked ridiculous in her sunglasses and hated seeing herself that way. She would never forget her sister's wedding, but for all the wrong reasons.

Common Characteristics of Abusers

Sometimes it's hard to admit that you're in a destructive relationship. You may think that the person you are with is

Drawing the Line

Alex Flinn, author of Breathing Underwater, *the ground-breaking young-adult novel on date violence, is also an attorney who has worked on domestic-violence cases. "When you're first going out with someone, you want to be together all the time," she says. "There's nothing wrong with that. But what about when a boy doesn't want a girl to have any other friends? What if he doesn't want her to spend much time with her family either? What if he tells her what to wear? Or gets mad when he sees her talking to another guy? This sort of behavior—controlling a girl, trying to keep hold of her—is an early sign of an abusive relationship. If a guy is treating a girl like this, she should break up with him. But if a guy sees himself in these statements, he ought to get help, too, so that he can have a better relationship in the future. Love doesn't have to be like this."*

just going through a difficult period and doesn't mean to treat you badly. No one knows precisely why some people abuse the people they care for most. However, research indicates that abusers share some common characteristics.

The Human Development and Family Science Division of the Ohio State University Extension notes that teens with a history of the conditions listed below may be likely to abuse their girlfriends or boyfriends:

- being abused or mistreated as children
- having witnessed violence between their parents, which encouraged their belief that date violence is acceptable
- alcohol or drug abuse
- exposure to community violence
- having aggressive friends

The Extension further notes that teens who abuse their dating partners may lack the necessary skills to resolve conflicts in healthier ways.

While these characteristics appear frequently in abusive individuals, it is important to remember that nothing is set in stone. Just because someone was abused as a child does not mean that he or she will be an abusive teen or adult. Some people turn out to be just the opposite. Others who find they have a tendency to be abusive get help and overcome the problem.

False Beliefs: A Foundation for Abuse

Other factors besides a person's family history or background can influence abusive behavior. How people see themselves and others is frequently a key factor. The same holds true for abuse victims. These individuals tend to have certain beliefs that keep them in destructive relationships. According to the

Alabama Coalition Against Domestic Violence (ACADV), young men who are abusive in their relationships often believe that:

- they have the right to "control" their female partners in any way necessary. This would include threats or actual physical violence.
- "masculinity" is physical aggressiveness. These young men believe that "real men don't cry." Showing any type of emotion is a sign of weakness to them. They equate being men with brute force.
- they "possess" their partner. They feel that the girl they are dating belongs to them much the way a motorcycle or a cell phone does.
- they should demand intimacy. Frequently such young men see this as their right—the idea is closely tied to their view of being manly.
- they may lose respect if they are attentive toward and supportive of their girlfriends. These young men are very image conscious. They would rather be "one of the guys" by being inattentive than experience the benefits of a truly close supportive relationship with a female.

How people see themselves and others is frequently a key factor. Abuse victims tend to have certain beliefs that keep them in destructive relationships.

Dating 101

Dating should be fun. A couple should be able to enjoy one another's company and the time they spend together. The University of Nebraska Cooperative Extension, which provides research-based education on various social issues, offers the following dating guidelines:

- **Dating partners are equals.** It's the twenty-first century. Girls do not have to be passive or obedient on dates. Young men should not control the dating relationship. Both people on the date should always remember that they are equals in every way.

- **Good communication is key.** People who date one another should be able to freely share their thoughts and feelings. Honest communication is vital to any good relationship.

- **Disputes should be settled through compromise.** No two people will agree on everything. When problems arise, they should be discussed. Any solution must consider the wants and needs of both parties involved.

- **Positive dating behavior is essential.** Dating partners need to exhibit high standards of behavior. Reckless and aggressive acts, such as drug use, spell disaster.

People who are dating are also entitled to mutual respect. It's impossible to build a healthy relationship without it. Haven House is a shelter for abused women and their children in Ontario, Canada. Its teen outreach program strives to prevent dating violence. The program defines respect as the following:

RESPECT IS...

...listening without interrupting

...taking your partner's feelings into consideration

...keeping an open mind

...agreeing to disagree

...trying to understand your partner's viewpoint

...loving yourself

...trust and honesty

...giving each other space

...nonviolence

...direct communication

...building a person up instead of tearing them down

...friendship

...not pressuring the other person

Young women who are date abuse victims often believe that:

- they are responsible for solving problems in their relationships.
- their boyfriend's jealousy, possessiveness, or even physical abuse is "romantic."
- abuse is "normal" because their friends are also being abused.
- there is no one to ask for help.

The Cycle of Violence

Date violence is not always easy to understand. You may wonder why someone in an abusive relationship breaks up with the abuser only to later take that individual back. People stay with abusive partners for a variety of reasons. Sometimes young women in these situations are influenced by old-fashioned gender roles. They wrongly believe that they have to "stand by their man," as the popular country-western song put it. They remain loyal regardless of the personal cost. Often these individuals refuse to see their relationships as abusive. Some think that they can't leave because their boyfriend needs them too much. Other girls think that they are nothing without a boyfriend and fear that they won't attract anyone else.

Many abused individuals suffer from low self-esteem. They think so little of themselves that they actually believe what their abusers tell them. They feel that they are to blame for their relationship's problems. Of course, none of this is true. But it is often hard to convince someone involved in an abusive relationship otherwise.

Abusive relationships tend to follow a cycle of violence. This is part of the pattern of abuse. Abusers are not always angry or mean. They can be extremely charming, giving their partners something to cling to. Some abused people think that if their boyfriends or girlfriends can be nice at times, they can always be that way. But in abusive relationships, the good feelings never last very long. When the slightest thing goes wrong, the abuser's anger flares up, and the cycle begins. Often the abuser takes out his anger on his partner.

Then, hitting and making threats allows the abuser to "blow off steam." These emotional explosions relieve the person's tension. The outbursts also trigger the cycle's final phase. During this phase, the abuser feels ashamed of how he or she behaved. That person once again becomes sweet and gentle. In some cases, the abuser may buy flowers or gifts to soften the partner's feelings.

If the abused person threatens to leave, abusers often become desperate. They will plead with the person not to go. Some may threaten to kill themselves, insisting that they cannot go on without their partner's love. Many will

The Cycles of Domestic Violence

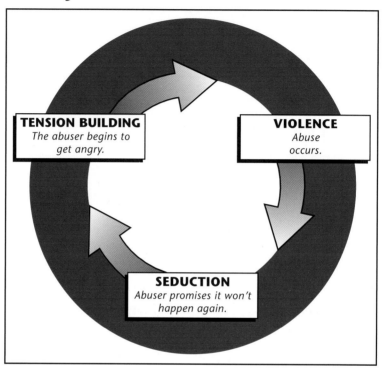

Many abusive relationships follow a cycle of abuse, which can happen repeatedly. Often, as time goes on, the "seduction" stage completely disappears.

cry like a baby at the thought of losing that person—even though just a few hours earlier, they may have brutalized their partner.

Unfortunately, all too often the abused person takes the bait. The abuser is forgiven, and all is well—for a little while.

But once a relationship has become violent, things tend to get worse rather than better. Hoping that someone will change has not been known to make it happen. Before long, the cycle begins again. Abusers know that they are free to frighten and mistreat their partners without facing any real consequences.

Once a relationship has become violent, things tend to get worse rather than better. Abusers know that they are free to frighten and mistreat their partners without facing any real consequences.

The blowups will continue because the abuser has not learned how to handle his or her feelings in a healthy way. By remaining in the relationship, the abused person unwittingly provides the abuser with an outlet. In the end, all the hitting and emotional abuse are more than just violence. They are about having power and control over another human being and the relationship.

Abuse victims are generally encouraged to leave potentially dangerous situations and get help. But the abuser has a responsibility to seek help as well. No one has the right to victimize his or her partner in a relationship. Physical, emotional, and sexual violence have no place in a loving relationship.

The Perfect Life?

Many young girls might envy the glamorous life of a beauty queen. But all that glitters is not gold. Pageant winners can become involved in abusive relationships as well. It happened to Carolyn Suzanne Sapp, who won the Miss America title in 1992.

Sapp, who is from Hawai'i, met Nuu Faaola in the late 1980s while making an appearance at an antidrug rally for young people. At the time she held the title of Miss Kona Coffee. Faaola, also appearing at the rally, was a handsome professional football player. That first meeting was the start of a whirlwind courtship filled with excitement and romance. The pair soon became engaged.

The situation did not remain ideal. Months later Faaola was cut from his football team, and he was clearly upset. He took out his anger and disappointment on the woman he planned to marry. One night while the couple was out walking, Sapp said something that annoyed him. He struck her, and she fell to the ground. Instead of helping her up, he repeatedly kicked her.

Sapp was shocked and hurt. She broke off their engagement, but her fiancé begged her to give him another chance. He told her how sorry he was and tearfully promised that he would never lay a hand on her again. Sadly, the beauty queen believed him and took him back.

Things were better for a while. Sapp's fiancé joined another football team, and once again the couple's future seemed rosy. But when Faaola was cut from the second team about a year later, his rage returned. This time it erupted while he and Sapp were riding in a car. At one point he tried to choke her with a seat belt. He also attempted to push her out of a moving car. Luckily Sapp was able to fight him off and safely stop the vehicle. But she wasn't safe yet. Her fiancé jumped out of the car and tried to attack her a second time, from the other side. Sapp sped away before he could open the door.

This time Sapp ended their relationship for good. When things calmed down, though, she agreed to still be friends with him. That

The Perfect Life? *(Continued)*

was a mistake. One night he called her from a bar claiming that he was too drunk to drive and needed a ride to a friend's house. Sapp drove him there, but when she got up to leave he tried to stop her. Seconds later he threw her against the wall and hit her. He also threatened her with a knife. Thankfully she was saved when the homeowner arrived.

The next day the beauty queen made her smartest move yet. She filed a restraining order against her former fiancé in the Hawai'i District Court. Now he could be arrested if he came near her. It was an important step for Sapp, one that would set the life of a future Miss America on a healthier course.

If you, like this former Miss America, date someone who threatens you with serious physical violence, you shouldn't ignore it. Nor should you call the person's bluff. A threat of violence is not funny. Individuals who threaten violence often carry out their threats. Talk to a responsible adult about the problem, but if that person says something like "boys will be boys," go elsewhere for help.

If you want out of the relationship and the person has threatened violence, the police department of Boulder, Colorado, suggests taking the following measures:

- Tell your parents, a friend, a counselor, a clergyman, or someone else you trust and who can help. The more isolated you are from friends and family, the more control the abuser has over you.

- Alert a school counselor or a security officer.

- Keep a daily log of the abuse.

- Do not meet the person alone. Do not let that individual in the car when you are alone.

- Avoid being alone at school, your job, or on the way to and from places.

- Tell someone where you are going and when you plan to be there.

- Plan and rehearse what to do if your partner becomes abusive.

Sixteen-year-old Lynn had been in an abusive relationship with seventeen-year-old Derek for nearly a year. At times he had shoved her, pulled her hair, kicked her, and hit her. Each time it happened, Lynn would say she was leaving, and each time she meant it. Once her family even got an unlisted phone number so that Derek couldn't call her anymore.

Unfortunately Lynn would weaken whenever Derek pleaded with her to take him back. Despite his past behavior,

Avoiding Abusers

One way to avoid an abusive relationship is to be alert to the warning signs. When considering dating someone, it's a good idea to find out:

- if it's a male, what his attitudes are toward females. Does he genuinely like and respect women?
- how he/she treated former girlfriend(s) or boyfriend(s). If he or she was abusive, chances are that the same will hold true for your relationship.
- how he/she deals with anger. Does he or she get into fights or engage in name-calling and put-downs? These are not good signs.
- if he/she keeps feelings tightly bottled up inside. Remember that good communication is essential for a healthy relationship.

she believed him when he swore that it would never happen again. Every time they made up Derek would buy her a stuffed animal. She had a room full of them, but they still didn't equal the number of bruises Derek had given her.

In some cases, the cycle of dating violence continues for years. And there are serious consequences for the victim. Severely abused people often do not reach their full potential. Frequently their grades drop, and they withdraw from healthy relationships with their friends. Some abused individuals develop eating disorders and become extremely depressed or anxious. Others engage in risky sexual behavior or become involved in substance abuse. There's another danger as well. People in violent dating relationships may end up with more than a broken heart. Some have suffered broken bones, concussions, paralysis, and even death. While abusive relationships may vary in some ways, nearly all follow the predictable pattern of the cycle of violence.

Three

Date Rape

K im was a high-school sophomore who dreamed of dating a college boy. She desperately wanted a boyfriend who had a car, lived in a dorm instead of with his parents, and could take her to exciting college parties. There was a college in the next town, and the local bus stopped on the campus. Kim convinced her best friend, Allison, to take the bus with her to the college library every day after school for about a month. They told their parents that they were going there to study, but they spent most of their time in the student lounge.

No one asked either girl out, but they did meet a boy who invited them to a party at his fraternity house. Kim and Allison were eager to go. They had no idea what they were getting themselves into. Neither had spent much time around boys older than fifteen.

When they got to the party, a group of boys ushered them through the fraternity house door. No one asked who they were, how old they were, or who had invited them. No one cared. It looked like the boys just wanted to have girls there. Kim and Allison were inside only a few minutes before a good-looking college junior struck up a conversation with Kim.

He told her that she was attractive and intelligent. Indicating how impressed he was with her, the young man said that he wanted to talk to her further but added that it was too noisy in the party room. He suggested that they go up to his room, where it was quiet. Kim agreed to go upstairs with the boy. He had been so polite that she felt he would not try anything.

She couldn't have been more wrong. When they got upstairs they sat on the bed because there weren't any chairs. Kim hadn't been there two minutes before the boy pushed her down on the mattress and got on top of her. Kim cried out for him to stop, but he said, "Shhhh...don't make so much noise. This will just take a few minutes, and then we'll really be close." As he continued to grope her, Kim kept protesting. He wouldn't listen. "You know you don't mean that," he said. "I can tell how much you like me."

Kim cried all through the rape. When it was over, she felt a mixture of anger, pain, and shame. As she slowly started to put back on the sundress that had been pulled off her, the boy lit a cigarette and said, "Just give me twenty minutes, and we'll have another go at it."

Kim burst into tears again. Incredibly, the boy seemed insulted. "Just get out of here then," he said. "You're no fun anyway. I'm going back down to the party to find a girl who wants to have a good time."

Kim was relieved to be able to leave. She went back downstairs but couldn't find Allison. She ran out the door and kept running until she reached the bus stop. She looked down at her dress and for the first time realized that the boy had stained it. At that moment, she hated both him and herself. As Kim stepped onto the bus, she had a terrible feeling in her stomach and wondered if she'd ever feel good again.

For a long time Kim blamed herself for what happened that night. Yet she was the victim, not the rapist. Unfortunately she'd met a young man who committed a crime and had the gall to be annoyed at his victim for not enjoying it. He needed to acknowledge what he did and take responsibility for it.

What Is Statutory Rape?

Statutory rape takes place when an older person has sexual relations with a youth. Statutory-rape laws were passed to protect young people from older predators. In cases of statutory rape, it doesn't matter if the young person consents. It is still considered rape because a young person is thought not to be mature enough to make that decision.

The age of consent, or the age at which an individual can lawfully engage in sexual relations, varies by state. It typically ranges from fifteen to eighteen years of age. So even if a nineteen-year-old boy and a sixteen-year-old girl agree to have sex, in states where the age of consent is seventeen or older, the boy can still be guilty of statutory rape. The girl's parents may press charges against him if they wish.

The National Crime Prevention Council suggests that young men monitor their feelings and behavior by following the suggestions below:

- Ask yourself how sexual stereotypes affect your attitudes and actions toward women.
- Accept a woman's decision when she says "no." Don't see it as a challenge.
- Avoid clouding your judgment and understanding of what another person wants by using alcohol and other drugs.

- Realize that forcing a woman to have sex against her will is rape, a violent crime with serious consequences.
- Never be drawn into a gang rape—at parties, at fraternities, at bars, or after sporting events.
- Seek counseling or a support group to help you deal with any feelings of violence and aggression against women that you may have.

Myths About Rape

Unfortunately, what happened to Kim is not uncommon. Kim was a victim of date rape, also known as acquaintance rape. Date rape is unwanted sexual intercourse with someone the victim knows. Some people still think that rape takes place only at knifepoint in dark alleys. Nothing could be more untrue. People have been raped at parties, in cars, in restrooms, and even in their own home by classmates, co-workers, and friends, as well as by strangers. A rapist can be young or old, rich or poor, and of any race or religion.

Some people still think that rape takes place only at knifepoint in dark alleys. Nothing could be more untrue.

While even the victims may not recognize date rape as rape, it is actually the most common form of the crime. The National Center for Victims of Crime reports that 683,000 females in the U.S. are raped each year; 80 percent of the rapes are committed by dates or acquaintances. According to the center, 13.3 percent of college women say they have been forced to have sex in a dating situation. The New York City Alliance Against Sexual Assault further reports that 8 percent of eighth- and ninth-grade students have reported being victims of sexual dating violence. These numbers do not take into account hidden rape—the large number of rapes and attempted rapes never reported to the police.

Though people often think of boys as the rapists in date-rape situations, boys have also been raped. Date rape occurs among gay and lesbian young people as well. However, same-sex date rapes may be among the most unreported. There's a reason for this. Gays and lesbians who report these crimes to law enforcement frequently feel that they are not taken seriously. Prejudice against homosexuals often interferes with the fact that a crime has been committed. According to the Student Health Services at Brown University, myths such as "women don't hurt each other" and "a fight between two men is a fair fight" can keep people from recognizing abuse.

Yet any form of rape is a crime. The person's gender is not an issue. It also doesn't matter if the rapist knows the victim, has dated that person before, or even previously had sex with the victim. Forced sex is always rape, and rape is always against the law.

Early Intervention

A 1998 Minnesota survey of more than 81,000 high-school students showed that nearly one in ten girls and one in twenty boys had been victims of date rape or other date violence. A separate 2000 study of five thousand South Carolina high-school students revealed nearly the same results.

Diann Ackard, a psychologist at the University of Minnesota who was involved with the Minnesota study, noted that date violence is a nationwide problem and that early intervention is critical to reducing incidents. "People always think about strangers and other adults when they think of the sexual abuse of young people and tend to forget about date-related experiences," she said. "This is another form of violence that we need to be on the alert for."

Another myth about date rape is that it is a crime of passion. Some people incorrectly believe that the rapist becomes sexually excited and is unable to control himself or herself. But rape has nothing to do with passion or love. Rape is a crime of power or control. The rapist wants to dominate the victim by forcing that person to have sex against his or her will. The rapist needs to feel in complete control of the situation.

Date-Rape Drugs

In recent years the risk of date rape as been heightened through the growing use of "date-rape drugs" such as Rohypnol (commonly known as roofies) and Gamma Hydroxybutyrate (GHB). These drugs, along with others like them, are fast-acting sedatives. At times rapists have slipped such drugs into the drinks of their unknowing victims at clubs or parties and various social events.

Rohypnol

Rohypnol comes in the form of small white round tablets that look like aspirin. The tablets are odorless and tasteless, and they quickly dissolve in drinks. The effects of the drug can begin within ten minutes and peak within two hours— though the effects can sometimes last for eight hours or longer. Rohypnol is prescribed as a sleeping pill in Europe and Latin America. It is illegal in the United States but is frequently smuggled into this country.

The National Women's Health Information Center notes that Rohypnol is regarded as a date-rape drug because "it can induce a blackout with memory loss and a decrease in resistance." The center further describes its effects: "About ten minutes after ingesting the drug, the woman [or girl] may feel dizzy and disoriented, simultaneously too hot or too cold, or nauseated. She may experience difficulty speaking and moving, and then pass out. Such victims have no memories of what happened while under the drug's influence."

GHB

GHB is sometimes also known as liquid ecstasy. It comes in the form of a grainy white powder or a clear liquid. The drug starts to take effect within fifteen to twenty minutes and reaches its peak effect in thirty to sixty minutes. The effects of GHB last only for about two hours. Some young people who've tried GHB say that it's like walking on a puffy cloud or having five drinks at once. The drug supposedly lifts anxiety and depression, making the user feel good—at first. Large doses can lead to a desire to sleep, slurred speech, drooling, twitching, vomiting, and passing out. When people are on this drug their eyes roll back, and they lose their gag reflex.

Like Rohypnol, GHB is illegal in the United States. The Drug Induced Rape Prevention and Punishment Act of 1996 was passed by Congress to increase the penalties for possession and distribution of these drugs. Under this law, anyone who distributes a controlled substance (illegal drug) to an unknowing person with the intent to commit a violent crime (including rape) can receive up to twenty years in prison.

Frightening Consequences

Drugs such as Rohypnol and GHB are particularly damaging to rape victims because they can cause partial or even complete memory loss regarding the events that occurred after the drug was taken. It is difficult for someone who has been raped to report the crime to the authorities if she or he can't remember precisely what happened. Because these victims are unable to provide the details necessary to secure convictions, their cases are frequently dismissed in court. Yet the victim is not any less traumatized as the result of the assault.

Drugs such as Rohypnol and GHB are particularly damaging to rape victims. It is difficult for someone who has been raped to report the crime to the authorities if she or he can't remember precisely what happened.

Wendy had heard at her high school in Miami that some boys had been slipping date-rape drugs into girls' drinks. That's why she was determined to be especially careful when she went to the first summer party after school let out. She even insisted on pouring her own Diet 7up into her glass.

At the party Wendy met a senior from a local private high school. He seemed so nice that it never occurred to her to take her drink along when she went to the restroom.

She should have taken it with her. The next thing Wendy remembered was waking up several hours later in the back of the boy's car with her skirt and underwear off. She had a splitting headache, and while she thought she'd been raped, she couldn't remember what happened.

Dating Under the Influence

It's obvious that date-rape drugs can lead to date rape, but other recreational drugs as well as alcohol can also cause problems. According to the Crime Prevention Unit of the San Diego State University Police (SDSU), "Dating under the influence of drugs or alcohol—as is driving—is very dangerous. The use of alcohol and drugs can and does compromise your ability to make responsible decisions and is often related to incidents of acquaintance rape. The majority of cases reported to the SDSU Police involved the excessive use of drugs or alcohol by both men and women." Unfortunately, the same holds true at high schools and colleges across the country.

If It Happens to You...

Date rape can happen to anyone. If it happens to you, it's important to know what to do. The National Women's Health Information Center has the following suggestions for individuals who have been sexually assaulted:

- Get away from the attacker to a safe place as fast as you can.
- Call a friend or family member you trust. You can also call a crisis center or a hotline to talk with a counselor. One national hotline is the National Domestic Violence Hotline, 1-800-799-SAFE or 1-800-787-3224 (TDD). Try not to feel ashamed or guilty, although such feelings—as well as being afraid and shocked—are normal. It is important to get counseling from a trusted professional.
- Do not wash, comb, or clean any part of your body or change clothes if possible. Do not touch or change anything at the scene of the assault; it is a crime scene.
- Go to the nearest hospital emergency room as soon as possible. You need to be examined, treated for injuries, and screened for sexually transmitted diseases (and if you're a female, for pregnancy). The doctor will collect evidence that the attacker may have left behind, such as clothing fibers, hairs, saliva, and semen. A standard "rape kit" is usually used to help collect these things.

- Call, or have the hospital staff call, the police from the emergency room to file a report.

Know Your Rights

The Women's Resource Center at the University of Utah further stresses that all date-rape victims—like victims of other forms of rape—have the following rights:

- to have a rape-crisis counselor accompany you to the hospital
- to call your personal physician to attend you
- to have privacy during the interview and the examination
- to have family, friends, or a rape counselor present during questioning and examination
- to have each procedure explained in detail before being administered
- to gentleness and sensitivity during the examination
- to an explanation of the reason for every test, form, and procedure
- to obtain available follow-up treatment and counseling

Individuals who have been date raped are crime victims. It is important that their friends and family treat them as such. The victims' friends can help the date-rape victim by believing her or him and offering their support. Sometimes this can be as simple as listening to and comforting the person, who needs a good friend now more than ever.

The use of these drugs is frightening for yet another reason. When mixed with alcohol or other drugs, they can be deadly. At times people have experienced very low blood pressure, slipped into a coma, and even died. In Michigan three boys were convicted of involuntary manslaughter and poisoning charges after slipping a large dose of GHB into a girl's drink. The girl, who was just fifteen years old, died.

The National Women's Health Information Center suggests the following to avoid being slipped Rohypnol or GHB:

- Be wary about accepting drinks from anyone you don't know well or haven't known long enough to trust. If you are accepting a drink, make sure it's from an un-opened container and that you open it yourself.
- Don't put your drink down and leave it unattended, even to go to the restroom.
- Notify other females you know about the effects of these drugs.
- If you think you have been a victim, notify the author-ities immediately.

Safe Dating

While everyone wants to have a good time when he or she goes out, it's important to be safe as well. Taking a few precautions can go a long way in preventing date rape and date violence. This can be especially important when going out with someone you might not know very well. The New York Alliance Against Sexual Assault suggests taking the following measures before going out:

- Tell your family or friends where you are going and when you'll be back.
- Memorize the telephone numbers of people you can contact or places you can go in an emergency.
- Keep spare change, calling cards, or a cell phone handy.
- Let family or friends know when you are afraid or need help.
- In an emergency call 911 or your local police department.
- Have money available for transportation if you need to take a taxi, a bus, or a subway to escape.
- Consider going out in a group with other couples.

If you ever start feeling uncomfortable in a dating situation, trust your instincts. It's okay to simply walk away. Remember, your safety comes first.

Surviving Date
Violence

t happened just as sixteen-year-old Mallory was leaving her house to meet her girlfriend at the mall. She heard a familiar sound—that of an old car in need of a new muffler—and a shiver ran down her spine. She knew it was Jack's car, and that meant that he was stalking her again. Jack was Mallory's former boyfriend, though her mother usually referred to him as their worst nightmare. During the five months he and Mallory had been together he had repeatedly hit and punched Mallory as well as forced her to have sex with him. The relationship finally ended after one terrible punch broke her nose.

Now Jack was in a court-ordered anger-management program. Mallory also had an order of protection, meaning that Jack wasn't allowed within a certain number of feet of her. But Mallory knew that people sometimes broke those court orders. Wondering if Jack had come to get even with her, Mallory forced herself to turn and look at the noisy car. To her relief it wasn't Jack after all—just another person in need of a new muffler.

The Aftereffects of Date Violence

Jack was finally out of Mallory's life, but she was still reeling from the effects of their relationship. Like many others who've been through traumatic experiences, Mallory was now dealing with the physical and emotional consequences of her harrowing months with Jack. This is known as post-traumatic stress syndrome, and it is not uncommon among people who've experienced date rape and severe date violence.

Mallory was surprised to find that she didn't immediately feel like her old self after she stopped seeing Jack. Instead much of the fear and anxiety she'd felt in the past frequently resurfaced. With post-traumatic stress syndrome certain triggers or cues in the person's surroundings can cause his or her anxiety level to rise. It might be a smell or a sound that brings back the old fear. In Mallory's case, it was the sound of a worn-out car muffler. When she heard it, she experienced the same terror she'd felt whenever Jack had come after her.

Mallory was surprised to find that she didn't immediately feel like her old self after she stopped seeing Jack. Instead much of the fear and anxiety she'd felt in the past frequently resurfaced.

Another common reaction is to keep reliving the trauma in their minds. It's like a tape of unwanted thoughts that keeps playing. Flashbacks and nightmares are common as well. During a flashback, the memory of the incident is especially vivid; the person feels almost as if it is happening again.

Grief and depression also frequently follow traumatic experiences such as date violence. The person may cry more easily than in the past and feel hopeless. At times the sadness can seem overwhelming. To make matters worse, many people begin to have self-doubts. They frequently blame themselves for what happened. In some cases, it becomes difficult for them to trust others again. They may feel that things are never going to be the same.

Post-traumatic stress syndrome isn't the only way that date violence can negatively affect people. Sometimes in trying to cope with their unsettling feelings, date-violence

Rape Trauma Syndrome (RTS)

Some date-rape victims experience Rape Trauma Syndrome (RTS). This is the name given to the various emotional responses that may result from rape. RTS has three phases:

The Acute or Impact Phase

The acute phase, which can last from a few days to a few weeks following the rape, can be an especially difficult time. It's important to remember that individuals have their own unique ways of handling stress. Some people will appear restless and irritable and tend to do a great deal of shouting, swearing, and crying. Others may seem unusually calm and quiet. During this phase, individuals may find it difficult to eat or sleep. Some people complain of continual nightmares about the rape.

Rape Victim Advocates, a nonprofit organization in Chicago, Illinois, described the acute stage as follows: "In general [the person's] initial response to the assault will be shock and disbelief. Many...may appear numb. Far from being inappropriate, this response provides an emotional 'time-out' during which the [person] can acknowledge and begin to process the myriad components of the experience.

[Someone] who was assaulted by an acquaintance may have a particularly difficult time overcoming the shock and disbelief. The experience of an acquaintance [or date] rape can also make a person question the trustworthiness of others in their life. If the assault was particularly terrifying or brutal, the [person] may experience an extreme shock response and completely block out the assault."

The Outward Adjustment Phase

In this phase, people generally resume their everyday activities but have not fully come to terms with the rape. They may suffer from depression and mood swings. Even if they say that all is fine, they usually don't feel fine inside.

The Resolution Phase

During the resolution phase, people learn to cope with what has happened. Though they may still have some of the same symptoms seen in earlier phases, they are starting to come to grips with the violence so that they can successfully go on with their lives. Ideally these individuals should be in professional counseling learning to better deal with what occurred.

victims engage in self-destructive behaviors such as unprotected sex and drug and alcohol abuse. Teen victims of date violence are also more likely to develop eating disorders. As psychologist Diann Ackard explained, "Disordered eating behaviors may be a way for youths who have been abused to project the painful experience onto their body. They punish their body for the abuse or try to manipulate their body into becoming unattractive to others."

Date violence is difficult for anyone to overcome, but it can be especially hard on young people. According to the National Center for Victims of Crime, adolescent dating violence occurs at a time when the young person is grappling with developmental and social issues such as peer acceptance, identity, and self-image. As the center's executive director, Susan Herman, noted, "Victimization can erode self-esteem and lead to deep feelings of helplessness, isolation, and despair."

Getting Help

Healing is possible, of course, but most people need help to do it. That's how Mallory finally began to feel better. For months after her relationship with Jack ended she claimed that nothing was wrong, even though she still felt upset. Finally her parents and friends convinced her talk to a professional about what she was going through.

Many communities throughout the United States provide services for both abuse victims and abusers. In recent years more people have realized that ending date violence is not just the responsibility of those involved in abusive relationships. Date violence is a community problem, and it is everyone's responsibility to work to stop it. As a result, many communities throughout the country are gathering their resources to fight it.

Ending date violence is not just the responsibility of those involved in abusive relationships. Date violence is a community problem, and it is everyone's responsibility to work to stop it.

In addition to providing counseling, many community organizations also educate people about date violence. Some have support groups where people who've been through similar experiences help one another to heal. Local domestic-abuse organizations and rape and sexual assault centers are often good places to find this type of aid.

Teenagers who are not sure where to go should ask a teacher, a guidance counselor, or a youth-services librarian to help them find community programs that work with teens. Among the most promising responses to date rape has been the creation of Sexual Assault Response Teams (SART).

In these community-based efforts, legal, medical, and sexual-assault specialists work together to assist the victim.

Perhaps the most important thing to keep in mind is that no one should ever be ashamed to ask for help. People who do are trying to improve their lives. They should be applauded.

Mallory found help at the teen unit of a free local counseling center that deals with rape and domestic violence. After working with her counselor, Mallory was better able to put her experience with Jack behind her and get on with her life. She regained much of her confidence and was ready to once again take charge of her future.

When a Friend Is Dealing With Date Violence

If you suspect that a friend is in an abusive relationship, encourage that person to get help. Unfortunately friends may be too embarrassed or ashamed to let even those close to them know what's happening. Therefore, it's important to be aware of the following signs of an abusive relationship:

- *Does the person have bruises that she or he can't explain?*
- *Is the person afraid of her or his dating partner?*
- *Has the person lost interest in things she or he once enjoyed (such as hobbies or being with friends)?*
- *Does the person apologize or make excuses for her or his dating partner's behavior?*

Legal Options

Date rape is a crime, and victims have the right to expect it to be treated as such. A victim can file charges with the police in the hope of having the case brought to criminal court. However, many cases never get to court because of a lack of evidence. Date-rape cases are hard to prove. If there are no witnesses or bruises, it frequently becomes a matter of one person's word against another's. Sometimes people choose not to press charges in a date-rape case because they don't want their private lives publicly aired in court. Many also don't want to relive the rape during the trial.

There are many good reasons to press charges, however. Some people say that it's important for them to have their day in court. They want to see that justice is done. Bringing rapists to trial also forces society to take the crime seriously, and it may prevent future rapes.

Victims can also sue their attacker in civil court to collect damages (money for physical, emotional, or other injuries). At times, fraternities have been sued if the rape took place at a fraternity party. If the rapist is underage, in some cases that person's parents may be sued.

Bringing rapists to trial also forces society to take the crime seriously, and it may prevent future rapes.

Don't Forget Your Rights!

The Women's Resource Center at the University of Utah stresses that date-rape victims should remember that they have the following rights:

- to report the attack to law enforcement and expect that all avenues within the law will be pursued to apprehend and convict the offender

- to make a report but not proceed with the prosecution

- to file a third-party report (for example, have a rape crisis center report the crime without disclosing your name)

- to do nothing

- to restitution (money for harm done to you) from the state violent-crime victims' compensation fund if you qualify

- to file a civil suit against the attacker

- to be treated during the investigation and trial in a considerate and sensitive manner by law-enforcement and prosecution personnel

- to ask if a female officer is available for the initial investigation if it would be more comfortable for you

- to have a friend, a relative, or another person of your choosing accompany you during all questioning or interviews

- to ask questions about aspects of the police or medical reports so that you understand their purpose

- to add or change your initial statement as you recall events more clearly

Women were further empowered when President Bill Clinton signed the Violence Against Women Act (VAWA) in September 1994. Under this law, violence against females is viewed as a gender-bias crime. As such, females can sue their attacker in state or federal court for violating their civil rights. If the woman wins the case, the attacker has to pay damages for the harm done to her as well as her legal fees. The act also contained other important provisions. More than a billion dollars was allotted to be spent on battered-women's shelters and to better educate judges and the general population on the effects of rape.

A Community Comes Together

Groups and agencies across the country are taking steps to reduce date violence. School districts in Massachusetts have been particularly active through the Teen Dating Violence Intervention and Prevention Program (TDVIP). The idea is to break the cycle of violence early on.

The Massachusetts Board of Education feels that the teen years are a critical time to do this. It stated: "Because dating is relatively new to adolescents, they are less likely to be entrenched in patterns of behavior, and more open to changing attitudes and behaviors, giving educators a unique opportunity to provide preventive education around teen dating violence, and to offer safe intervention strategies within the school."

The program exposes students to assemblies and performances stressing the importance of mutual respect in dating. There are also mini-courses taught by young people who are former abuse victims or former abusers. These students help train other students to identify abusive behaviors. Other topics they explore include communicating with dating partners respectfully and constructively working through conflicts.

Stand Up and Be Counted

Teens can take a stand against date violence. Among the many ways to do so:

- *Talk to a guidance counselor or a parents' group about holding workshops at school on date violence. Suggest that a peer-education program on teen date violence be started.*
- *Create bulletin boards in the school cafeteria, halls, and classrooms to increase awareness of date violence.*
- *Consider putting on a skit or play about date violence.*
- *Volunteer at a rape crisis center.*
- *When you see TV programs that condone or glorify violence against women, write to the network and program sponsors to protest it.*

In addition, the project sponsors weekly counseling groups for young male abusers. Both school staff and police officers receive special training to handle teen violence, and in some areas twenty-four-hour hotlines and professional counseling services have been established. The Teen Dating Violence Intervention and Prevention Program of Massachusetts has been used in public middle and high schools throughout the state as well as some areas in Canada, New Zealand, and Australia.

Because males are more often the abusers in date-violence situations, many programs focus on helping them to change their behavior. Men Overcoming Violence (MOVE) is one such endeavor. MOVE uses counseling workshops and theatrical presentations to help high-school and middle-school youths in "mastering new skills and changing attitudes and beliefs to end violence." In San Francisco, the organization even offers weekly workshops for youths incarcerated in juvenile jail. Because many of these young people are there due to violent behavior, it's important that they are exposed to better ways of dealing with things before returning to the community.

It's crucial that people everywhere take a stand against date violence. The problem is too widespread and detrimental to today's youth to ignore. October is National Dating and Domestic Violence Awareness Month, and groups often sponsor special events then. One especially moving rally, sponsored by the group Voices Against Violence, was held at the University of Texas in Austin. After an evening of stirring stories and songs about surviving date violence, those in attendance took time out to remember the individuals who couldn't be there that night. These were the young people who died as a result of this brutal crime.

Flowers were placed on seventeen empty chairs. Each chair bore the name of a young victim who died in Texas as the result of a violent relationship. "This affects all of us," one of the students at the rally noted. "I'd be really shocked if there is anyone in the audience who hasn't had to deal with this, not just personally but through a friend or in some other way." Perhaps Voices Against Violence coordinator Geeta Cowlagi best summed up the driving force behind this movement when she said, "This is everyone's problem."

Glossary

battered: repeatedly hit, beaten, or otherwise physically abused

coalition: a group of people or organizations that have banded together to achieve a common goal

compromise: to accept something that wasn't quite what you wanted in order to reach an agreement

concussion: a head injury caused by a violent blow

consent: to willingly agree to something

cycle of violence: a pattern of violence that includes tension-building, violence, and apologies date rape: unwanted sexual intercourse or other sexual acts with someone the victim knows

date violence: physically, emotionally, or sexually harming one's partner in a dating relationship

detrimental: negative or damaging

domestic violence: violence or abuse between people who are married, living together, or dating

dominate: to control or master

emotional abuse: insults, threats, humiliation, and yelling to frighten or intimidate someone; emotional abuse also occurs when individuals try to control their partner's movements, destroy his or her property, or isolate him or her from family and friends, making the person feel powerless and alone

intimidate: to frighten someone through threats and violence

order of protection: a court order requiring an individual to remain a predetermined distance from a particular person

paralysis: partial or complete loss of movement in a part of the body physical abuse: bodily harm such as pinching, restraining, kicking, choking, pushing, shoving, slapping, biting, burning, and hair pulling

post-traumatic stress syndrome: a disorder that can occur following the experience or witnessing of a life-threatening event; it often includes reliving the event through nightmares or flashbacks, difficulty sleeping, and feelings of isolation

Rohypnol (roofies): sometimes called a date rape drug, this is a fast-acting sedative that can cause drowsiness, confusion, and temporary memory loss and that can immobilize an individual, rendering that person less able to stop a rape; GHB, another common date rape drug, has similar effects

sedative: a medication used to calm nervousness or emotional turmoil

sexual abuse: the use of force to engage a person in sex or sexual behavior against his or her will

statutory rape: when an older person has sexual relations with a youth

traumatized: having endured a physical or emotional injury resulting from force or a severe emotional shock

Further Resources

Books

Abner, Allison and Linda Villarosa. *Finding Our Way: The Teen Girls' Survival Guide.* New York: Harper Perennial, 1996.

Bandon, Alexandra. *Date Rape.* New York: Crestwood House, 1994.

Bode, Janet. *Voices of Rape.* Danbury, Connecticut: Franklin Watts, 1998.

Dee, Catherine. *The Girls' Guide to Life: How to Take Charge of the Issues That Affect You.* Boston: Little Brown, 1997.

Hicks, John. *Dating Violence: True Stories of Hurt and Hope.* Brookfield, Connecticut: Millbrook Press, l996.

Johnson, Scott A. *When "I Love You" Turns Violent: Abuse in Dating Relationships.* Far Hills, New Jersey: New Horizon Press, 1993.

Levy, Barrie. *In Love and In Danger: A Teen's Guide to Breaking Free of Abusive Relationships.* Seattle: Seal Press, 1998.

Mufson, Susan, and Rachel Kranz. *Straight Talk About Date Rape.* New York: Facts on File. 1993.

Rosen, Marvin. *Dealing With the Effects of Rape and Incest.* Broomall, Pennsylvania: Chelsea House, 2002.

Winkler, Kathleen. *Date Rape: A Hot Issue.* Berkeley Heights, New Jersey: Enslow Publishing, 1999.

Organizations

National Center for Injury Prevention and Control
Mailstop K65
4770 Buford Highway, NE
Atlanta, GA 30341-3724
776-488-1506
www.cdc.gov/ncipc/default.htm

National Center for Victims of Crime
2000 M St. NW, Suite 480
Washington, DC 20036
202-467-8700
www.ncvc.org/ncvc/Main.aspx

National Crime Prevention Council
1000 Connecticut Ave. N.W., 13th floor
Washington, DC 20036
202-466-6272
www.ncpc.org/

The White Ribbon Campaign
365 Bloor St. East, Suite 203
Toronto, Ontario, Canada M4W3L4
416-920-6684
www.whiteribbon.ca/

Online Sites

The Corporate Alliance to End Partner Violence
www.caepv.org

Deana's Fund: Acting to Prevent Violence
www.deanasfund.com

The National Women's Health Information Center: Violence
Against Women
www.4woman.gov/violence/index.htm

National Organization for Women
www.now.org

National Sexual Violence Resource Center
www.nsvrc.org

New Hope for Women—Teen Dating Violence: What You
Need to Know
www.newhopeforwomen.org/teens.htm

The Pennsylvania Coalition Against Rape
www.teenpcar.org

Rape, Abuse & Incest National Network
www.rainn.org/

The R.O.S.E. (Regaining One's Self-Esteem) Fund
www.rosefund.org

The National Center for Victims of Crime: Teen Victim Project
www.ncvc.org/tvp/

Index

About the Author

Award-winning author **Elaine Landau** worked as a newspaper reporter, a children's-book editor, and a youth-services librarian before becoming a full-time writer. She has written more than two hundred books for young readers. Ms. Landau has a bachelor's degree in English and journalism from New York University and a master's degree in library and information science from Pratt Institute. She lives in Miami with her husband, Norman, and her son, Michael.